THE CREDIT TRAP

THE CREDIT TRAP

Anthony Clinkscales

ISBN: Hardcover   978-1-4257-6719-8
             Softcover   978-1-4257-6697-9

To order additional copies of this book, contact:
Xlibris Corporation
1-888-795-4274
www.Xlibris.com
Orders@Xlibris.com
41518

CONTENTS

DEDICATION TO MY FAMILY

Thank you for your love and support.
May God continue His abundant blessings upon you
and may His principles for economics and wealth
continue to be a guide in your financial walk!

ACKNOWLEDGEMENTS

Thank you, God,
for allowing Your Holy Spirit
to guide me in writing this book.
Only through Your grace and direction
was this made possible.

To the world's greatest wife:
Thank you, Margaret,
for always standing with me.

FOREWORD

I used to own a business that helped people restore and improve their credit.

During the process, I realized two things commonly occurred:

1. Some creditors weren't paid.

2. As soon as their credit standing was improved, some people fell right back into the credit trap.

This went on for years and, finally, it dawned on me that I was correcting a problem only to see a number of people drop immediately back into debt. A lot of debt. I realized that most people didn't really understand credit or the credit trap system, and how it is designed to keep people in debt!

I learned a valuable lesson. But I also knew there had to be a better way to correct credit mistakes and financial problems for people everywhere. Over many years dealing with finance and credit, I discovered some basic truths, and I want to share my thoughts, concerns and accomplishments with you.

I know that everything that has happened in my life has not just been a coincidence. All of it has been purposed! My experiences with finance, money and credit has brought me to write this book on how to get out, stay out, and avoid the credit trap—and live a victorious financial lifestyle!

I believe that the more knowledge and understanding a person has about finances, fewer problems will be encountered. So as you read this book, I urge you to absorb what it's saying and make the necessary changes to free yourself from the chains of the credit trap!

INTRODUCTION

Your ability to enjoy life can be ruined for a very long time if credit is used improperly. The GET IT NOW and PAY LATER attitude will put you in financial bondage that will destroy your dreams for an abundant lifestyle. Credit should be used *only* as a last option and not because it is available to you. In fact, credit should be avoided at all cost, whenever possible!

The credit trap is a system designed to lure you into continuous money borrowing that will trap you financially. If you fall into it, you will be literally forced into living a defeated, debt-burdened lifestyle.

Don't be fooled by the world's system; once you obtain the knowledge and principles for financial independence, credit *must* be avoided! The only way to get out of trouble is to stop borrowing money *immediately*. Be content not to further extend credit and develop a plan to pay all your creditors off for good. At the same time, start developing a plan to increase your cash and cash flow. As your debt decreases, your wealth will increase so you can live a debt free life.

Credit has become a must-have thing in this world, and people are destroying their lives trying to get more of it just to satisfy their immediate wants. People have been led to believe that there is security in the world's system, but that's why banks, savings and loans, credit unions, finance companies, credit card companies, and other moneylenders are in control of all the wealth!

How can you have dominion if you owe every Tom, Dick, and Harry? You must understand that you were not created to be financially defeated (the borrower). Instead, you were created to have dominion and authority (the lender)!

Becoming the lender is not an overnight task. Deuteronomy 28 says it shall come to pass if you follow all of God's commands. This tells us that there is a process to becoming a lender and not a borrower. Now, as you journey with me, I want you to discover your divine purpose in life, owing no man anything but love!

CHAPTER ONE

SOLVING THE PROBLEM BEFORE IT BEGINS

It starts with teaching your children right now about credit and financial responsibilities. Don't wait for the banks, credit card companies, finance companies and other loan institutions to do it for you. All they want is to get you and your children so deeply into debt you'll have to depend on them for the rest of your natural lives.

The world's way is to control your finances to keep you and your children from living an abundant and prosperous financial life. It's called the credit trap, and it is designed to keep you in debt forever!

The time is *now* for you to break this cycle of debt and live in the abundance that Jesus came to give you. If your children see you borrow money for everything, they will think it's okay to do the same. The bible says to train your children in the way he or she should go. You *must* show them that living debt-free is the way. I know you can't be debt free instantly, but the choices you make today can create a better future for you and your family.

Attain victory *now* over your finances so that the world you live in cannot hold you back! You must learn and teach your children how to manage their money so they won't have to live paycheck-to-paycheck, as so many people are doing right now. If you don't train them, you are just setting them up for financial failure, which will result in their falling into the credit trap.

Don't let your children make the same mistakes you and I did. Solve the problem now. Start with yourself first, because there is always room for improvement. Begin to budget and manage your money better now. And make some wise investments that will give you a good return on your money. Don't let your children learn the hard way when it comes to money. Remember, the word says to train your kids they way they should go.

Avoiding the credit trap is a must for the next generation. And getting out of the credit trap is a must for you! You can't obtain the wealth from the wicked by continuously borrowing money. I'm not saying a person will never have to borrow money, but I *am* saying either you believe God's word or you'll stay in debt for a very long time. In other words, you *must* develop your plan of escape from the credit trap today!

Major credit problems can begin as early as when a teenager graduates high school and enters college. This is when our children are most vulnerable and most likely to be introduced to credit, such as financing their education by getting a student loan. Don't let your child be a victim.

There are too many young men and women who have graduated from college and, five years later, are still paying for their education. Does this make any sense? The answer is NO, and that's why you must change your and your children's mindset concerning money and finance.

Learn to make money work for you instead of you working for it! Start a college education investment plan—not just a bank account, but an investment that will yield a good return—so when your children are ready for college it won't be a burden to send them.

What about the danger of pre-approved credit cards? High school grads don't even have a job and they are already receiving credit card offers. It happens every day as they step onto college campuses everywhere. Credit card companies line up to give teenagers a line of credit to put them in debt. This begins a trend in young people's minds to GET IT NOW and PAY FOR IT LATER! We have to train our children in the way they should go, not the way the world is training them!

Can you imagine how the words "pre-approved" sound and feel to 18-year olds about to enter college? They don't even have a job! Actually, I don't have to imagine it because I was there once, and it sounded and felt really good.

But now I understand it was only a trick of the enemy to get me to conform to this world's system and, ultimately, to fall into the credit trap with major debt hanging over my head!

Friends, stop letting the enemy destroy you and your kid's financial lives. Learn to follow truth and not feelings. Feelings tell us it's fine to borrow money because it makes you feel good instantly. A teenager about to enter college will love the instant gratification. But truth says to you and me to be a good steward. Save for the future! That's your job as a parent.

Start a college investment fund for your kids and put it where banks would invest *their* money. Stop letting banks use your money to make a profit for themselves! How do you think these banks can loan out so much money and not go broke? It's because they are investing the money you deposit with them into a system that will yield big profits to them.

Banks only give you 1%, 2%, or maybe even a 4% return if you are a "good customer," while they are earning 10%-30% on the money you give them. Have you ever heard of the Rule of 72? It means if you divide the interest rate into 72 it will tell you how many years it will take your money to double. If the banks are giving you 2% and they are making 24%, then you tell me who is making and getting all the wealth.

Here's an example of the Rule of 72: If you're making 2% interest, divide that number into 72. The answer is 36, meaning that your money will double in 36 years. So if you have $1,000 in the bank earning 2% interest, it will become $2,000 in 36 years. What a waste of your money!

That same bank will invest that $1,000 you put into their savings plan and get 24% interest! Divide 24 into 72, and you'll discover that your money will double for the bank *every 3 years*. That same $1,000 will become $4 million in 36 years . . . but all you see is $2,000! How can this happen?

It's simple. God says His people suffer because of the lack of knowledge. God didn't say His people suffered because of the lack of money. He said because of the lack of knowledge!

One of the greatest things ever discovered in this world is compound interest! The faster your money doubles, the more it will grow!

Examine this chart:

RULE OF 72
Example

2% divided into 72 = 36 years
Money doubles every 36 years

24% divided into 72 = 3years
Money doubles every 3years

0 = $1,000
36 = $2,000

0 = $1,000
3 = $2,000
6 = $4,000
9 = $8,000
12 = $16,000
15 = $32,000
18 = $64,000
21= $128,000
24= $256,000
27=$512,000
30=$1,024,000
33=$2,048,000
36=$4,096,000

Which do you prefer?

Even if you received just 12% return on your money, it would still double every six years!

Now it's up to you. Learn, practice this simple technique, and teach your children to do as you do when it comes to the principles of money. Take control of your finances today. Say this out loud: "No More Debt and I Must Invest!"

Think about your life financially. Now ask yourself, do you want your children to grow up making the same financial decisions you did? If you answered "no" to that question, you must immediately stop this enemy called the credit trap before it destroys your life and your children's, as well.

Stop the problem for your kids before it begins!

The way a person thinks when it comes to dealing with credit and debt is a major issue. If you tell yourself that you can get a product or service with no money out of your pocket and that you'll pay for it later, your way of thinking is leading you into the credit trap and setting you up for failure.

You bet you'll pay for it later, and that's for sure! BIG TIME! More stress, more headaches, and more money given away in interest and payments. This is the world's way of doing business—from the White House to your house—and it's a mistake!

Our nation has been corrupted by debt and has fallen into the cycle of the credit trap—and it's only getting worse! The United States of America is trillions of dollars in debt and our government still thinks it's perfectly okay to borrow, borrow, borrow.

But what about you? What are *you* going to do? Are you just going to settle for life as you're living it in debt, or are you going to use the knowledge offered in this book to make your life and your children's lives better in the financial arena?

Doing the right thing when you're used to doing the wrong thing can be tough to change. And change can be fearful. But that's why God gave you a measure of faith! As you read and hear the word of God as it relates to prosperity, wealth and more abundant life, you must believe what the word says and take action.

Resist debt and it will flee. Invest, and wealth you will see!

Remove your old way of thinking right now. And when situations arise and your money is low, you must begin to speak, meditate and stand on God's word. You must use the power and knowledge He gives you.

Don't be your own worst enemy. Tell yourself that failure is not an option, that money is coming because you are following and living His commands and principles. Get your thinking in order and show yourself through your faith to be worthy of the increase in wealth that's sure to arrive. Let your *works* prove your faith.

God has plans for you! Good plans! Plans for you to prosper! God is waiting for you to activate the power that works in you. It's there, God planted it inside of you when you received salvation! Think positively about what you need to do and make the change for yourself and your children so you can live a better lifestyle.

Here are five things you can do to get out of debt and keep your children out of the credit trap:

#1. Be a good example.
#2. Budget, and show your children how to budget.
#3. Tithe, give and sow seeds and teach your children to do the same.
#4. Save and invest, and teach your children how to save and invest.
#5. **Stop borrowing money!**

CHAPTER TWO

BREAKING OUT OF THE CREDIT TRAP

You may not be able to pay off every debt you owe today, but you can find the vision to do so. Remember, as a person thinks in his or her heart, so is he or she. You have to begin to see yourself out of the credit trap, out of debt right now—even as you are reading this. Faith is knowing and believing you have it inside you to speak about the unseen and then to see it. Faith is having confidence that it will come to pass as long as you do the works to get it.

If you've been thinking "Get it now and pay later," you must change this mentality immediately! Remember, you have to follow truth and not feelings. **Stop charging just because it feels good. Begin saving so you can pay cash with no payments attached. Do both and feeling good will be a continuous lifestyle.**

I know that nothing happens overnight. However you can make up your mind that you will not continue to buy things on credit, and that includes your kids' education. Remember the truth that says if you follow God's commands it shall come to pass that "YOU WILL NOT BE THE BORROWER!"

You have to start climbing your way out by not borrowing. You must evaluate where you are *right now* and take action to get where you need to be. Write down what you need to do to get out of the credit trap. It's not enough to just think it. Write it as a visible reminder.

If you don't have a vision of being out of debt, you won't have the motivation to get out of debt. A vision is something you can see, and that's why it's called a "vision!" You have to see where you are to get where you want to go!

As you write, say to yourself, "I have life and I have it more abundantly. I am the head and not the tail. I will no longer be a slave to the lender. I am living a victorious financial life, and God is bringing me into my wealthy place!" You can say this when you know you're headed in the right direction financially. You can have this if you write the vision and have a plan.

Debt is your enemy. There is no other way to say it. It will put you in bondage by making you think more about your financial problems than the promises of God. **But I declare today that the debt of the credit trap will no longer hold you captive**! Breaking out of the credit trap can be a reality. Get serious and make up your mind to believe that whom the Son has set free, he or she is free, indeed. Receive it in your heart and move into your true destiny for yourself and your family!

Borrowing has been implanted in our minds. I say this because people are in so much debt from thinking about how they can get things quickly. But it's time to change your life for the better. Remove the chains that hold you in debt bondage and replace them with God's word of financial freedom! Don't allow the cycle of debt to rule you any longer. It is your right to be free; it is your time to be free; you were purposed to be free!

God has plans for your life, and being a victim of the credit trap is not one of them! Who have you placed your faith in, anyway? Money or God? If it is in money, you're probably in debt up to your ears right now. That's why you have to change directions.

Don't just continue to go along with the flow of things. Create your own flow: A cash flow! Begin to create and generate other income streams. Don't just rely on your job for a paycheck every week.

Get out of your comfort zone. Do something you have never done so you can get something you've never had! Use your power and let God's principles get you out of debt and into your wealthy place!

Remember, God doesn't give you money. He gives you the knowledge and power to get the money. I haven't read anywhere in the bible where it says "I will give you a hundred dollars!" Have you? I didn't think so. It's your job to get all the wisdom and knowledge and apply it powerfully to get the results you want. What can you do right now to make extra money to get your head above water? Think about it. There are hundreds of things you can do legally to generate a financial increase.

The world's system will lead you deeper into the credit trap. That's what it was designed to do. Operating according to God's principles will lead you out of the world's system. If you're not a born-again Christian and you want to be, I believe that this is a good place for you to stop and say, "God forgive me of all my sins. Jesus come into my heart. I believe that you are risen from the dead. You are my savior, and I want to be saved and live according to your word!"

If you offered this prayer with sincerity, the power of the Most High God is now working on your behalf and helping you break out of the credit trap and overcome other obstacles in your life. It can be done in Jesus' name! Seek God first and His righteousness and all these things will be added unto you. This includes your wealthy place. And let me tell you that wealth means more than just money! It means having everything *good* in your life!

I don't know about you, but to me, there is nothing good about being in the credit trap!

The credit trap will take you places you don't want to go to. I'm reminded of the people coming out of Egypt, wandering in the wilderness and trying to get to the Promised Land. Because of their complaining and lack of faith it took them 40 years to arrive and, even then, only a few made it.

Those few who believed were overcomers! The others? Instead of following God's instructions, they just complained about where they were, made a bunch of excuses why, and died in the mess they themselves created.

If you keep complaining and making a bunch of excuses, the credit trap will do the same to your finances. It will keep you captive and you may never see your financial abundant place. You must follow God's instructions by being faithful, managing your money well by budgeting, tithing, investing wisely, and giving cheerfully. And then you will receive an increase.

The Promised Land is meant to be a land of plenty! The credit trap is the land of lack and poverty! It's a circle of credit and debt that will keep you from your true destiny. It will lead you in a path of continuous borrowing and get you deeper in debt. Stop complaining about where you are and get a plan to get out of the wilderness!

Think about the money you've already spent on interest and repayments in your life. This is money that could have been saved for college education, a new car, your wedding, honeymoon, even a home. I am talking about paying cash for your wedding and honeymoon! Cash for a new car! Not financing it! Stop complaining and wishing for things to happen and start saving so you can pay cash!

The first car ever built was not done on a wish. It was built by:

#1. Having a plan.
#2. Putting the plan into action.
#3. Determining to finish the job.

You have to do more than just wish you were out of debt. You have to **do the works** to get what you believe!

Are you just sitting around waiting for it to fall from the sky? Are you waiting for it to grow on the tree in your back yard? Well guess what? I've been there, done that, and it's not going to happen that way! There is inner power waiting to work on your behalf so you can live an abundant, wealthy lifestyle! To break out of the credit trap you must get up, get a plan, and do the works to ensure your plan succeeds.

Remember, the word of God says that He will bless everything you put your hands to, but you've got to put your hands to something! If you do nothing you'll get nothing, but if you do something you'll get something.

If you are saying to yourself, "I can't pay cash," stop it! Watch what you say. There is power in your tongue. Don't be your own worst enemy. Get that old way of thinking out of your mind and out of your mouth right now! Let your words be a motivator in your life.

Speak positively! Say, "I can pay cash!" Say, "I am **not** the borrower!" Say "I am prosperous!" Say "I will make some money today!" Say "I am out of the credit trap and I will make my money work for me and not make me work for it!" Your words have the power and ability to make things happen! What do you *want* to happen? Do you want to be in debt all your life or do you want freedom from debt?

Look back at your past for just a few seconds, as a way to make your future brighter. I want you to think about all the money you've spent on payments and interest in the past three years. Now think about the past five years. How about this past year? What if you had saved that money? Would you be better off right now? Sure you would. I know you can't change the past, but you have a decision to make right now!

Debt burden or Debt freedom! The choice is yours!

Start taking the necessary steps today to break out of the credit trap and into the freedom and promises of God. Start paying things off immediately, beginning with the smallest debt to the largest *(see debt acceleration, chapter 9)*. And if you don't already have a savings and investment account, start one today even if you can only save and invest $5 or $10 a week.

As time passes and bills are paid off, increase your savings and investment amount and before long you will have more than enough to begin a new life of paying cash! Be patient and diligent and I promise you your efforts will pay off.

Proverbs 10:4 says that he becometh poor that dealeth with a slack hand: but the hand of the diligent maketh rich. Get out there and make something happen! Get out of your bed, out of your house, and jump-start your destiny! *YOU* HAVE TO MAKE THINGS CHANGE!

So mark your place and put this book down if you need to, and go get your inheritance **right now!** Just do your part and God will do His!

There is a price to pay for progress, but the results will be priceless!

CHAPTER THREE

WHAT DOES THE CREDIT TRAP
REALLY WANT?

The credit trap only wants one thing: Interest, interest, and more interest. The world's system lives for it and gets wealthy off of it. Remember the Rule of 72? The lending institutions make money when you deposit with them and when you borrow from them. So it's a double win-win situation for them.

Interest is the amount you pay above the amount you borrow. And when people constantly borrow, hundreds, thousands and even billions of dollars in interest are given away each year. Just one mortgage loan of $100,000 at 7.5% interest will give the bank, over 30 years, a profit of more than $150,000. And that's if you never refinance. If you do, the interest starts all over again. How many times have you refinanced? Scary isn't it?

No wonder the saints can't get the wealth that's laid up for them, we are too busy giving it to the world. Stop using the world's system to get what you want and start using the knowledge of God and His principles to get what you need. Don't accept what the world's system has to offer; it's just a plan for the enemy to keep you trapped!

Have you heard the saying, "Good credit, bad credit or no credit?" It's everywhere. This is what they advertise to lure you in. But it doesn't really matter what type of credit you have because when you buy on credit, the credit trap gets more of your money.

Look at it this way: the more you finance on credit equals more interest paid. It doesn't matter what your credit looks like. Don't be fooled by your credit worthiness, because it's only a trick to categorize you and make you think you're getting a good deal.

It's true that if your credit worthiness is good, you get a lower interest rate. And if it's bad you receive a higher interest rate. But good credit or bad, any way you look at it, you are still falling into the credit trap of this world's system. Your job is to get out of debt as quickly as you can—and stay out!

Here's how the system works. This is a standard car loan analysis for borrowing $25,000 dollars at 7.5% for five years.

Analysis	
Amount Financed	$25,000.00
Annual interest (e.g., 8.25)	7.50
Duration of loan (in years)	5
Start date of loan	
Monthly payments	$500.95
Total number of payments	60
Yearly principal + interest	$6,011.38
Principal amount	$25,000.00
Finance charges	**$5,056.92**
Total cost	$30,056.92

You pay $5,056.92 dollars in interest! You gave away $5,056.92 of your hard-earned money! If you had saved your money for 5 years to pay cash *you would have* an extra $5,000.00, plus interest, on your money right now! YOU would have it, not the bank!

What about a $100,000 house at a 7.5% interest rate for 30 years?

Analysis	
Amount Financed	$100,000.00
Annual interest (e.g., 8.25)	7.50
Duration of loan (in years)	30
Start date of loan	
Monthly payments	$699.21
Total number of payments	360
Yearly principal + interest	$8,390.57
Principal amount	$100,000.00
Finance charges	**$151,717.22**
Total cost	$251,717.22

You will pay $151,717.22 in interest!

You'll pay more money in interest than the amount you financed on a 30-year mortgage. The world's system is designed to get as much money as it can from you and keep you in debt. I have good news for you, though. You have power over the enemy. So if debt is your enemy you have power over debt!

Being in debt because of the credit trap means you're not living the life that Jesus came to give you. The bible tells us that it shall come to pass that you are the lender and not the borrower as long as you follow God's commands. It's your job to owe no man anything but love. Start believing and living your life according to the words of God! And apply the knowledge you've learned and are going to continue to learn to get out of debt!

Why should you continue to live in the path of need, debt, and being broke? Stop thinking you have to borrow money to get what you need and want. If you choose to finance your first home, that doesn't mean you have to pay interest on it for 30 years. Get a plan to pay it off early. Pay extra toward the principle of your loan and/or make split payments.

Example: If your mortgage payment is $800 a month, pay $400 every two weeks. Not only will this technique allow you to pay your mortgage off early, it will save you thousands of dollars in interest. By paying this way, more of your money goes toward the principle of your loan, not to the interest. Plus, it accelerates your payoff time!

Interest that you pay on money borrowed can be used better in the kingdom of God. Malachi 3:10 says that if you bring all the tithes into the storehouse so that there will be meat in His house, God will open to you the windows of Heaven and pour out a blessing so bountiful that you won't have room enough to receive it all!

By bringing your tithes into the storehouse you give God the opportunity to bless you by increasing every area of your life—including your money! You will eventually have more resources to live an all-cash lifestyle, to help other people, and to leave an inheritance for your children and their children, also.

Remove the thought of borrowing money from your mind unless it's your own money you're borrowing. Debt and credit should not be in your vocabulary.

You have to start from somewhere, so you might as well start in your mind and heart. Start thinking about wealth and abundance and a cash-paying, cash-living lifestyle. As a person thinketh, so is he or she. Begin changing the way you think right now! Don't give the enemy what it wants. All those interest payments can be avoided!

Jesus has already paid the price for your success! He's already won the battle! According to Psalm 66:12 God will bring you into your wealthy (abundance) place! Men have ridden over your head long enough. You've been through the fire and through the water, and now it's your time to make a change and receive your abundance! Receive it! And have it!

Start preparing to break the cycle that has been a curse over your life for so long. Just as we are preparing ourselves spiritually, we must also prepare ourselves financially. Stop giving the enemy what it wants and give God what He deserves. God did not intend for you to be a credit-trapped Christian. God intended for you to be a free and abundant, prosperous-living Christian.

Christians often focus on spiritual increase (*which is good and necessary*), but hardly ever focus on financial increase. Why do Christians think it is okay to be in debt and praise God anyway? It's not okay! God's word clearly says **"Beloved, I wish above all things that you prosper and be in health, even as your soul prospers."**

Do you see that the word of God says, above all things He wants you to prosper! Not above all things, be in debt. God is a good God, a giving God, and a God who wants you to have great increase in every area in your life, money included!

If you're going to use credit, use it to buy a foreclosed house to fix up and resell. For example: Buy a house for $40,000, put $5,000 in repairs and sell it for $60,000. You just made a $15,000 profit. Will this help you to get out of the credit trap? Sure it will. And you can do this over and over until you achieve financial independence. This is just one way to increase your cash flow, and there are plenty of other ways, too.

The green light has been given for you to increase yourself financially. Use your dominion and make up your mind right now that you will break out of the credit trap! You can live the prosperous and victorious life that has been given to you. But you have to do your part first.

Your financial preparation will open doors of financial greatness!

CHAPTER FOUR

DESIGNED TO KEEP YOU IN DEBT

It is not God's fault that this world is living in debt bondage. It's that old way of thinking that people are accustomed to. It is the world's way of doing business. You know, get it now and pay for it later.

This way of doing business has led us into so much debt that the thought of being debt-free is crushed as soon as it enters a person's mind. That's why the credit trap must be stopped and a new way of doing business must be planted in your mind. Getting out and staying out of debt should be your new goal!

The world's system is designed to keep you borrowing and borrowing, driving you into living just a little beyond being broke. That's right, the world's system is designed for you to be in debt forever and to put you in subjugation to it. The world's system is not your friend!

The world's system may say to you, "Renew your loan if you're having trouble making payments." It may say "Consolidate your bills into one easy monthly payment." It sounds good, but the odds are against you.

Chances are you may re-open your previous loans which will put you deeper in debt. The lender may say, "Don't worry if you can't make this month's payment; we will defer (extend) this payment to the end of your loan." All of this is making it longer for you to pay off your loans. It is designed to keep you in the credit trap forever. Don't do it! Don't give in! Stop borrowing money!

How about renewing your loan when it is almost paid off? Does this sound familiar? It does to me. I remember when debt controlled me. When debt decided what I must do. Debt made me work longer and harder and work jobs I couldn't stand just to keep my head above water.

Peter 2:19 says a man is a slave to whatever has mastered him. I was in debt bondage and it seemed like I couldn't climb out. The love of money had become my worst enemy and I was sinking fast. I started with a dream of being wealthy, but ended up in a nightmare of being broke.

Everybody dreams of being financially independent, but I had allowed the credit trap to conquer me. I was sucked in by what I thought was the answer to my dreams of becoming financially independent. It was a long time before I realized that the world's system was not on my side, it was my enemy.

Don't misunderstand me, it's not the person loaning you the money who is evil. It's the evil spirit of this world that's your enemy. You see, we wrestle not against flesh and blood but principalities in high places, evil spirits that are against you becoming debt-free.

At one time, I was so deep in the credit trap that I began to think there was no way out. I was overtaken by debt bondage and had a spear in my heart crushing my dreams of being debt-free and financially independent. I was a Christian, but I was in bondage because of my wrong thinking and wrong choices. I woke up one day and realized I had truly fallen deep into a hole of debt and stress, better known as the credit trap.

I had nowhere else to turn, I was up to my ears in debt. I told myself that there had to be a better way, and if I was a son of God I had to have my financial freedom back! I started reading and believing Psalm 66:10-12, words that changed my outlook on life! I began to put myself into scripture and believed that God was talking directly to me. I then changed my way of thinking and made a decision to climb out of the credit trap, one bill at a time.

Working two and three jobs and accepting all the overtime I could get, I pushed toward coming out of debt and into my wealthy place. Every day I thought to myself that I was becoming debt-free and that God was bringing me into my abundance. Yes, my wealthy place! Not just money, but freedom from stress, worries, and the chains of the credit trap that were trying to hold me back.

I begin to notice a positive change in my finances. I was tithing consistently and giving cheerfully, and God opened the windows of Heaven to me. I was paying things off and not just paying on them. Some release from the credit trap was finally here and I began to see the light at the end of the tunnel. I kept God first and continued my journey toward my goal, and things continued to get better.

I remained faithful in my tithes and offerings to God and committed myself to a plan of financial freedom. As time passed, the credit trap was no longer in control! I had paid off several debts and my head was finally above water. It wasn't over yet, but at least I could pay my remaining bills in the same month they were due.

I still wasn't satisfied with just being able to pay on time. Something inside of me demanded total freedom! God's word had been rooted in me; NO DEBT was what I wanted! I was determined not to be the borrower!

I pressed on, seeking the mark of the higher calling touching my finances. And before long, using the desire and endurance God had given me to achieve my goal, I had every debt paid off.

Hallelujah!!! I was debt-free and had defeated the credit trap in my life! I was no longer a borrower! Instead, I am now the lender! And I owed nobody anything but LOVE!

When you're in debt you are in bondage! There is no freedom in bondage. You are a slave to the one you owe. The credit trap is designed to control you, hold you, and ultimately it will try to destroy you. I truly believe that the credit trap is straight from the devil because people become depressed, stressed out, get divorced, they cuss, fuss, and are often very sick because they have borrowed too much money!

If the credit trap has lured you in, stop believing that the world's system is okay. It's not. It's against you and it wants to destroy your life and your children's lives, too. Put the GET IT NOW and PAY FOR IT LATER attitude out of your mind and life.

You have to get sick and tired of being sick and tired, and you must make a change. I'M ASKING YOU TO PLEASE MAKE THAT CHANGE TODAY, SONS AND DAUGHTERS OF GOD! If you don't, you will always be a slave to the lender. Make up your mind that you will owe no man anything but love. This is the way God intended for His people to live. Get your finances in order today and begin to pay off what you owe. It may not be easy at first, but greater is He that is in you than he that is in the world!

Work hard to accomplish your goal and begin to pray over your debts to be paid off in the name of Jesus! When Jesus died and rose on the third day, He overcame all death! Physical death! Mental death! Spiritual death! **And yes, financial death, too**!

That's good news, because you no longer have to be dead financially! You can break out of the credit trap and enter into your wealthy place because Jesus has already defeated debt! God's system is designed to give you abundance and a successful lifestyle!

CHAPTER FIVE

GOOD DEBT OR BAD DEBT?

While having no debt should be your ultimate goal, there is such a thing as good debt. Which do you have: bad debt or good debt? Understanding the distinction between them will make a huge difference in your ability to get out of the credit trap.

Bad debt is when you borrow money for something that depreciates in value or does not bring you a return on your investment. This is the type of debt most people have. Some examples are financing a television, clothes, tires for your car, furniture for your home, and gas on a credit card. All are depreciating assets; the longer you have them the less valuable they become.

Think about this: Why would you pay $3.00 a gallon for gas, charge it on a credit card, and then pay 15% to 20% interest on top of that? That $25 dollars worth of gas ends up costing you $35-$45 dollars, or more, depending on the interest rate. What a waste of your hard-earned money.

The reality of bad debt is that when you borrow money for things that depreciate in value you are setting yourself up for financial failure. If you fill your tank with gas using that credit card, chances are you will still be paying for that same tank of gas months later, even though the gas was used up in a week's time. How about those tires you bought two years earlier with that credit card? Have you ever heard the term "burning rubber?" Well, you've been burning more than rubber. Just as the treads on your tires are fading away your money is going up in smoke, also!

Good debt, on the other hand, is when you borrow money on something that generates a return on your investment. An example is real estate, which is one of the best investments a person could choose, an investment which has been proven to increase in value over a period of time. Anything you finance that can be sold for more than you paid may be considered good debt. Even buying a car at wholesale and reselling it at retail is okay. Using your credit to start a new business that makes you a profit is acceptable.

There are plenty of opportunities to put the power of time and money to work on your behalf. The problem is that some people simply don't take the time to seek those better opportunities. They are so lazy that, instead of using the power within them, they would rather sit back and hope that money will fall out of the sky. We don't live in a fairytale world. If you want something better to take place in your finances and your life, it's up to you to do something to make it happen.

CHAPTER SIX

WILL A MAN ROB GOD?

Are you robbing God? Is prosperity and abundance working in your favor? Are you a Christian who is always struggling, sick, broke, busted and disgusted? *If so, you may be robbing God!*

You are a child of the Most High God. Yet some of us steal from our own Father and anyone who does so is cursed. The word of God says you are cursed with a curse because of your lack of tithing and giving. Why would you rob your own Father when He wants to give you an abundant life?

You must turn from your wicked ways and acknowledge God. Stop robbing Him and He will heal your land, the land of milk and honey (abundance and prosperity)! God's plans are designed to give you a successful lifestyle.

We are sons and daughters of God. We come from abundance and more than enough. That's our origination. He knew us before we entered our mother's womb. There is no lack, no poverty, no sickness, and no boundaries in God. He is more than enough! He is life and He gives life more abundantly. Stop robbing your Heavenly Father in your tithes and offerings and He will restore your wealthy place!

Satan is a thief who lost his privileges a long time ago. And now he's trying to steal your relationship with God. Satan wants you to be just like him. He wants you to be defeated. He wants you to live in bondage. He wants you to be evil and a thief like him.

But you were made in the image and likeness of God! That's why you have to stop robbing Him. He created us to be His sons and daughters, and a true son or daughter shouldn't rob their Father.

Is your ego too big to acknowledge the Most High God with your tithes and offerings? Look at the word EGO. It could mean you have *Edged God Out* in your money. By breaking the covenant of tithing it leads to a curse on your finances and in other areas of your life. God says return unto Him!

In order to live abundantly in your finances you must allow God to break the curse. Return to God a *minimum* of ten percent of your increase. Tithe and give and watch the windows of Heaven be opened. Pour out a blessing that you want have room enough to receive it all!

God has pleasure in the prosperity of His servants! He wants you free and not bound. To have, and not to lack! He wants you to prosper in every area of your life! It pleases God to see you prosper in your health, in your spirit and in your money!

But many of you are living the opposite of what the bible says, and then you wonder why you can't get what is promised to you. It's simply because you must return to the biblical principles of wealth. And it begins with your tithe and offering. The tithe is one-tenth of all your increase and gain in your life. How can God trust you with wealth if He can't trust you to tithe? You have to follow God's plan first, and then you will get your part of the wealth that belongs to you.

We have a right to be wealthy, to be prosperous and to live abundantly because we were created to have dominion! You are a part of God, joint heirs, and His spirit lives in you!! A portion of God's abundant wealth is waiting on you but it can't be released until you are found trustworthy in the money He's already giving you.

Stop robbing God! Don't say things like, "I can't afford to tithe," or "I'll just give what I have left over," or "God doesn't need my money." Guess what? If God doesn't need your money then you surely don't need His!

It's not that God *needs* your money, it's about being in a covenant relationship with Him. God already owns it all! The Earth is the Lord's and the fullness thereof. That's right! He owns it all, and all the money, too. This is your Father and He is loaded, and I do mean LOADED! And guess what? You're a part of His family. Simply put, you inherit what He has when you grow up and follow His instructions!

Following the world's system leads to the credit trap. Following God's system will open the windows of Heaven in your life—and it's waiting to be opened to you right now!

God is trying His hardest to get abundance and wealth to you, but your lack of tithing and offerings are keeping the financial windows of Heaven closed.

Here's how you can unlock God's wealth into your life!

#1. Honor God in your money.

Malachi 3:10 says that God will open to you the windows of heaven and pour you out a blessing that you won't have room enough to receive it all if you tithe. This is a commandment that must be implemented in your Christian walk to break the curse and unlock financial prosperity. Do this faithfully and the results will be tremendous!!!

#2. When you give, you should always give with a cheerful heart.

God loves a cheerful giver! Don't give for the sole purpose of needing your light bill paid. He knows your needs, so *whatever* you give must be done cheerfully!

When you give, God's word will come true in your life when He says in Luke 6:38, Give and it shall be given unto you good measure, pressed down, shaken together, and running over, shall men give into your bosom, for with the same measure that ye mete withal it shall be measured to you again. God will **multiply** the giving back to you if you give and give cheerfully!

#3. Speak it.

There is power in your words. You must begin to change the atmosphere around you with words of wealth and prosperity. Begin to say things like "I am rich, I live in abundance, I'm a son/daughter of the Most High, the windows of Heaven are open in my life, and I live in the favor of God. You are what you say you are and you can have what you say you can have! So go ahead. Speak it!

#4. Expect it.

Trust God. Expect His words to come true in your life. If you don't have faith in the unseen, you can't have the unseen! In other words, if you can't see the picture in your mind of the windows of Heaven being open to you, they won't be. If you don't expect yourself to be free from debt, you won't be. If you can't see your new home and expect to have it, you won't have it.

You have to expect God to do what He said He would do after you have done what you're supposed to do! Have faith in the unseen and expect to have it! Expect it to be pressed down, shaken together, running over and given unto you after you have given! Expect it, and God will allow your part of His abundance to come into your life!

#5. Have a plan.

Get a plan of action *right now* to get out of the credit trap and start receiving your wealth. God will not overflow you with His abundance unless He knows you are in position to receive it and your motives for it are right. You may receive a small portion of it, but not an overflow of abundance unless you are positioned.

Why would God give you hundreds, thousands, millions, or billions of dollars if He knows your plans are not good for it and/or you are not positioned to handle it? Sometimes our intentions are good but our actions are bad. God knows what He can trust you with, based on your past examples. Prove to God you are ready by getting your house in order and setting good examples. And then your plan will be accepted for your abundance.

#6. Have Faith.

It is impossible to please God without faith! Have confidence that it will work for you. Do your works and know without a shadow of doubt that God will bring you into a wealthy place!

God cannot lie, if you are a faithful tither the windows of Heaven have got to be opened in your life!

CHAPTER SEVEN

DEFEATED BY FUTURE PAYMENTS

Future payments can be defined as payments you have to make continually, month after month, until the amount of money borrowed has been paid in full, plus interest.

Future payments are not fun. In fact, they can be very depressing. The credit trap controls your financial future when you have continuous payments. Knowing that the money you earn is spent before you get it should make you want to step on and crush the spirit of debt. The thought of making payments on something for many years should spark something in you that says, "Enough is enough!"

The credit trap's desire is to keep you making payments forever. To keep your back against the wall. Haven't you had enough? Aren't you sick and tired of being defeated by payment after payment and then by more payments? Don't you want your future to be free from making payments to others?

If nothing changes, nothing changes. Change your way of doing things today. Stop borrowing money just to pay it back later. Make a brighter future for you and your family. It's time you make up your mind to end future payments and start enjoying your life and your money.

Do you know of any older retired people right now who are still making payments on something? Perhaps it could be your aunt or uncle. Maybe your next-door neighbor. Or even your parents. After retirement, they have to get a part-time job just to make ends meet. This is not right. It's happening, but it's definitely not right.

Who wants to be working at the local supermarket after retirement? In order for this not to happen to people, year after year, the credit trap must be stopped! Setting yourself up for future payments must come to an end. Lives are being destroyed and the credit trap is getting bigger and fatter.

Not borrowing money is the only way to avoid these future consequences! The credit trap wants all it can get from you. It knows no name. Don't give in any longer; your life and your children's lives depend on it.

There is light at the end of the tunnel. With determination and faith you can defeat future payments. Here are two steps you can put into action *right now* to conquer future payments.

#1. Add extra money to your monthly payments and make sure it is applied to the principal of your loan. This will accelerate the payoff of your loan(s).

#2. **STOP BORROWING MONEY!!**

Follow those two simple steps and, before long, future payments will be a thing of the past!

UNCONTROLLABLE DEBT

Uncontrollable debt is debt that has gone haywire in your life. It is when you thought all your monthly bills were paid but another bill comes due. It is when you get past-due notices on some bills while other bills still need to be paid. If you don't know when your bills are due and you can't keep track of whom you owe, that's uncontrollable debt.

Uncontrollable debt will push you into living from paycheck to paycheck, literally making your financial dreams fade away. Living from paycheck to paycheck will eventually lead you into robbing Peter to pay Paul and stealing from Janet to pay Jane. And if you don't get it quickly under control it may lead you into robbing your friends, your church, and your family just to make ends meet.

Uncontrollable debt will keep you from living a victorious financial life. It will give you unwanted stress and burdens. The spirit of debt wants you to think that in order to enjoy life you must continuously borrow money. That's a lie! Jesus came so that we might have life and have it more abundantly, even in our finances.

The truth is: *You* are the lender, not the borrower! *You* must stop and re-adjust your finances. *You* must get in control of the bills even if you have to get a second job! *You* must take a stand and renew your mind immediately!

The enemy is not playing around, he wants you destroyed and out of his way. And if he has to do it from a financial standpoint, he will. So many people are falling by the wayside because they have too many payments stressing them out. They can't get to God because of the pressure of the credit trap!

You have to budget yourself and cut out those things that are not necessities. Drop your pride and pick up your faith! Sometimes you have to go down to come back up the right way. The old way of thinking and the bad patterns to which you're accustomed will only lead to a future of continuous, uncontrollable debt.

Renew your mind and take charge of your financial future today! Don't avoid your debts, this will only make maters worse. Face what you have. Get your plan of action together and put it in motion. Uncontrollable debt is not the American dream, it's the American nightmare. Why should you continue to live in this nightmare of debt? Why?

Here are two simple things you must do to stop uncontrollable debts.

#1. Write *all* your bills down on paper in the order they come due. As you pay them, check them off as "paid" for that month. Do not go 30 days late on any payment. If you don't have enough money to make all of your monthly payments on time in a given month, get a second income to make ends meet.

#2. **STOP BORROWING MONEY!!**

Take control of your future by controlling your money!

CHAPTER EIGHT

BROKE NO MORE!

I am convinced that conforming to the world's system will keep you just a little above being broke. The credit trap has no respect for any person. It will have you living from paycheck to paycheck forever. What kind of life is that? Who in their right mind wants to live from paycheck to paycheck all their life? It's exhausting to know that, before you even get paid, the credit trap has already accounted for your money.

Being a slave to debt has got to become a thing of the past!

Don't misunderstand what I am saying. You may have to borrow money for a house, but you **should not** borrow money for things like a new TV, bed, clothes, tires for your automobile, and etc. And you should really try your best to save your money to pay cash for a vehicle. And that house should not take thirty years to pay off!

It is the continuous financing of lots of things that leads to being broke. Think about it? A $400 TV on credit? An $800 bed on credit? What are you thinking? Why should you watch and sleep your money away in monthly payments and interest?

Discipline yourself and save for these types of purchases. I know it's easy to say "charge it" and pay it off later. But one debt leads to another when it's that easy. Before long you'll have several different amounts to pay for and instead of paying them off, they'll just get paid on.

This is where you are conforming to the world's system and falling into the credit trap. The cycle of being in debt has been birthed and you begin living from paycheck to paycheck, stuck for what seems like forever in the credit trap.

Breaking out and not being broke anymore begins with a plan to make your money work for you. Start saving to pay cash for your purchases. And if you do borrow money for a house or car, create a plan to pay it off early.

Think about this: If you buy a $10,000, $20,000, or even a $50,000 car, how long will the bank finance it? Three to six years, right? But if you buy a house they want to finance it for 30 years. Why? Because all they want is your interest.

But, if you can pay a $50,000 car off in five or six years, you can pay off a $50,000 house in the same length of time. Even if the house costs $100,000, it doesn't mean you have to pay on it for 30 years.

Knowledge is power, so think about it! Why not pay your house off early? Who says you have to have a 30-year mortgage? Not God! It's the way the banks have designed it for you. The world system is designed to keep you in debt and just a little above broke. Getting all your interest and payments and keeping you subjugated is how the credit trap operates. The credit trap is designed to keep you in debt and below the bar.

You have to be willing to take a stand. Do what you know is best for you in your finances. Turn from the world's way of doing things and come out on the right side. God says if you return unto Him he would heal your land. That's right, the land that you're in right now can be prosperous!

The credit trap will call your name just as long as you let it. It sounds good to only have a $50 payment on something. But, in reality, you end up paying $900 for that $400 TV because of the "easy" $50 credit trap payment!

Put the GET IT NOW and PAY LATER attitude out of your mind; it will destroy your dreams of being debt-free. Not being broke takes discipline and determination. You have to take control and stop financing everything. Forget about wanting to have everything right away. Be patient and anxious for nothing. Save your money and pay cash. Don't let debt cause you to be broke anymore!

Broke no more! Save and pay cash for it!

CREDIT CARDS

What are credit cards?

Credit cards are those pretty plastic square shiny cards that fit easily and firmly in your pocketbook, your wallet, and in your hand. They're the instruments by which people charge their purchases. They look so good and they're so tempting, aren't they?

But wait a minute. Did you know that credit cards are the most widely used form of credit-trapping a person? The average credit card debt in America is around $20,000 per family. Those pretty little plastic cards are deadly to your financial life.

Don't be fooled by this form of debt. Credit cards will send you straight into the credit trap rapidly! Credit card companies compete to sell you their money on credit cards. Oh, yeah! One says, "Use mine anywhere you go," and the other may say "It's like putting money in your wallet," and still another may say, "You get cash back every time you use it." That sounds like a sales pitch to me. But I urge you not to fall for that trick.

Here's how they work . . . and here's how you are trapped:

Let's say you accept a credit card offer and the card issuer starts you out with a $3,000 credit limit. You begin to charge things on your credit card: clothes, groceries, lunches, gas, you name it.

And then you say to yourself, that was so easy I think I'll charge something else, something more expensive—like furniture. So you acquire some furniture you always wanted, on credit, and now you're good to go, right? Well, not really. You are now operating according to the world's way of doing business, which is: "Buy Now, Pay Later!"

And then you go into a gas station and, instead of taking the time to go inside to pay cash, you pay at the pump. With your credit card. And then you leave the gas station and remember something you don't really need but have always wanted. And since you have your pretty, new shinny credit card, you say to yourself, I can GET IT NOW and pay for it later. Before you know it, you've charged your entire limit. That pretty little shinny credit card has just caused you to become a victim of the credit trap conforming to this worlds system.

Then you say to yourself, "I will pay off my credit card when the bill comes in." About 30 days later, the bill comes in with a $3,000 balance and you notice that the credit company has offered you a minimum re-payment plan. Let's say it's $45 a month. You are so excited and you tell yourself, "I can keep my $3,000 and only pay $45!" WOW, what a deal!

I know what you're thinking: Your other bills are due anyway, and you were wondering how you were going to pay for them as well as your new credit card bill, too. You think you just got a sensational deal of only a minimum payment due.

Let me enlighten you about what you really got. Of that $45 minimum payment, approximately $37-$41 goes directly to paying interest only! Instead of your balance going down to $2955, it is being paid down by about $6 (depending on the credit card) to $2994.

And it gets worse. Almost all credit cards are based on revolving interest, which means interest is added *daily*. That's why, when you make a minimum payment on a credit card, you owe about the same amount when your next monthly statement arrives. All they want is your interest! The world system is banking on you settling for the minimum re-payment plan to keep you in the credit trap forever.

The trap deepens when you receive another letter in the mail that says, "You are pre-approved to receive another credit card. This time it offers a $5,000 limit, and you say to yourself, "Great! This is a way to pay off my other credit card and have some money left over."

So you fill out the application and you receive your next new shiny card. You pay off your other credit card and with the $2,000 remaining limit you do just what the credit trap wanted you to do. You charge it! The GET IT NOW and PAY LATER attitude has just caused you to get deeper in the hole.

Then the bill comes in on your new credit card and what do you do? As most people are currently doing, you pay the minimum payment. You were already programmed to pay minimum payments so the credit trap can keep you in debt.

Month after month you make the minimum payments because it's so convenient or there is no extra money available to pay a higher payment because of your other financial obligations. This is what happens when the credit trap rules your life. That's why you have to make up in your mind to change the way you do things right now. Don't charge it, save to pay cash for it!

Credit cards are a waste of your time and money and they should be avoided at all cost. It can take as long as 20 years to pay off a credit card balance of $3000 if you are only making minimum payments!

> **Don't let the excitement of a convenient, pretty, plastic card ruin your life!**

CHAPTER NINE

DEBT ACCELERATOR

There is a way to pay off all your debts quicker and get back in control of your money. It's called Debt Acceleration.

Here's how it works:

Step #1. Take the smallest debt you owe (not the smallest payment, but the smallest *balance*). Add $50 a month to your normal monthly payment. If you can pay more, do it. Make sure the lending institution applies all of the extra payment to the principal of your loan and continue doing this until the debt is paid in full.

Step #2. After the bill in step #1 is paid off, take both the additional $50 and the normal monthly payment from that first bill and apply it to the payment of the next highest debt. Pay that additional money every month until the bill is paid in full. Make sure this extra money is applied to the *principal*. With the additional money added to this monthly payment you should have this debt paid off in less than three-fourths the normal time and maybe sooner (depending on how much you owe)!

Step #3. After the second debt is paid off in step #2, reward yourself! Go out for dinner and a movie. Or buy yourself a new pair of shoes, a new outfit, or something else that's fun for you. Once you have rewarded yourself, start a savings account if you don't already have one.

Step #4. Resume your debt acceleration on the next highest financed bill. Bring over the monthly payment you were paying in step #2, along with the additional $50 or more, and add it to these monthly payments. Don't stop until this third debt is paid in full.

EXAMPLE: #1

	Balance	*Payment*
Debt 1.	$ 800	$200 monthly (John Doe Finance)
Debt 2.	$ 6,000	$ 80 monthly (Credit Card)
Debt 3.	$ 2,500	$150 monthly (Personal Loan)
Debt 4.	$ 14,000	$425 monthly (Car Loan)
Debt 5.	$ 28,000	$380 monthly (Second Mortgage)
Debt 6.	$125,000	$750 monthly (First Mortgage)

You would start with Debt 1 because it has the **smallest balance**. **Not** with Debt 2 because it has the smallest payment. Remember, when that debt is paid you always continue with the next **smallest balance** and not the smallest payment.

EXAMPLE: #2

Step #1—Debt 1 ($800) = $200 normal monthly payment plus additional $50; pay until paid in full.

Step #2—Debt 3 ($2,500) = $150 normal monthly payment, plus the extra $200 you now have from paying off debt 1, plus the additional $50 until this one is paid in full.

Step #3—Reward yourself and start a savings account if you don't already have one.

Step #4—Resume the debt acceleration with Debt 2 ($6,000), $80 normal monthly payment plus the $150 and the $200 from the other debts that are paid off, and the additional $50, and apply all to this or most of it to this monthly payment.

Keep in mind that this is money you were already spending. The only extra payment is $50! As you can now see, you've freed an extra $350, plus the $50. After a few months of making these payments, you can skip one month to take a little breather, but only if you're disciplined enough to start paying the additional amount the next month. Remember, your goal is to be *completely debt free*!

Step #5—Go to the next smallest debt, bring over the extra money and apply it to the monthly payment. Continue until you have the deed to your house!

With the additional monthly payments you are applying to your debts, your car can be paid off in approximately half the time you expected—not five or six years—and your house won't require 25 or 30 years of payments for you to get the deed!!!

While you are going through the debt acceleration process, remember to make sure the additional monthly money is applied directly to the *principal* of your loan. And start a savings plan, even if its only $50 a month. After your debts are paid off, increase your savings amount with a portion of the money you have freed (perhaps 15% to 20%). Ultimately, you will begin paying cash for what you need and want and the credit trap can no longer hold you captive!

CHAPTER TEN

BUDGETING

A budget is a guide or plan to control your spending and to give you discipline in your finances.

Here is an example of a budget chart you can use.

MY BUDGET   MONTH_____

CREDITOR	PAYMENT	DUE DATE	CHECK IF PAID	PAID OFF	NOTES

Use the percentage guidelines below to see if you are staying within your budget. You may wish to use the higher percentage if your income can bear it.

Example: $3,000 a month net income times (x) 30% for housing = $900 available for that expense.

1.	Tithe	10%	
2.	Housing	30% -	35%
3.	Food	15% -	20%
4.	Auto	15% -	20%
5.	Insurance	3% -	5%
6.	Debts	0% -	8%
7.	Entertainment	5% -	8%
8.	Clothing	3% -	5%
9.	Savings	5% -	15%
10.	Medical Expenses	4% -	8%
11.	Miscellaneous	4% -	8%

God wants us to have a plan. Mathew 25:21 says, "His lord said unto him, well done, good and faithful servant; thou hast been **faithful** over a few things, I will make thee the ruler over many things: enter thou into the joy of thy Lord."

How can you have the joy of the Lord, and have life, and have it more abundantly, if you don't have a plan? Being obedient is better than sacrificing. Paying your bills and paying them on time is more honorable to God than buying 5 new gospel CD's when you know the finance company has been calling you for a late payment for the last three weeks.

Can God trust you to pay your debts and pay them on time? Can God trust you in preparing a plan to get out of debt? Or will you just blow your money on nonsense and say it was worth it, I had to have it?

Sure, we all need music of praise to get us through rough times, but timing is everything. It won't hurt you to listen to your favorite gospel station for a few months—instead of buying new CDs—to help you get your praise and worship on!

Think about the men with the talents. To one He gave five, to one He gave two, and the other received one. The one who had one did not have a plan to make a difference with what he had. He made an excuse for not using his talent to bring forth an increase and was punished for it (Mathew 25:24-25).

What I am saying is that planning is a major step in avoiding the credit trap. Planning gives you an avenue to start prospering and live abundantly. If you fail to plan, you plan to fail. And this is what happened to the person with one talent. It doesn't matter how much you have, what matters is what you do with what you have!

Living below your means is **not** a bad thing. If this is what it takes for you to climb out of the credit trap, then do it. Don't be afraid to go below your means a little bit, because when you come back up you will be stronger and more successful than ever!

Satan's desire is to control your mind so he can control your money. The CREDIT TRAP knows no name. It is your job to prepare yourself with a plan to get out of debt and to stay out!

THE LOVE OF MONEY

The love of money leads to a defeated and sinful lifestyle. The love of money will put you deep in the credit trap and make it seem like you can never come out. The love of money will make you think you can borrow your way out of debt and into abundance. But it doesn't work that way.

Financial abundance is obtained through planning, hard work, discipline, and sound principles. You have to be rooted and grounded in principles that work to get the results of an abundant financial lifestyle. It is God's will that we have more than enough, but we have to seek Him first and not the money.

Is your treasure (money) where your heart is?

1. DO YOU THINK MONEY IS THE ANSWER TO ALL YOUR PROBLEMS?
2. DO YOU TITHE?
3. DO YOU HELP PEOPLE IN NEED?
4. DO YOU CONTINUALLY BORROW MONEY?
5. DO YOU HORDE MONEY?
6. ARE YOU STINGY WITH YOUR MONEY?
7. DO YOU GIVE CHEERFULLY?
8. ARE YOU SHARING YOUR MONEY WITH YOUR SPOUSE?

9. DO YOU THINK ABOUT HOW YOU CAN GET MORE MONEY FOR SELF GRATIFICATION ONLY?
10. ARE YOU FAITHFUL IN WHAT GOD HAS ALREADY GIVEN YOU AND MANAGE YOUR MONEY WELL.

Don't let the love of money control you. Renew your mind. Ask God to let your mind be like the mind of Christ! Remember that the earth and the fullness of it belong to God. It is your responsibility to seek God first and His righteousness and all your needs and wants (including money) will be added unto you through your planning and obedience!

The *love* of money is the root of all evil.

CHAPTER ELEVEN

THE POWER OF TIME

Time may be defined as a continuous period measured by clocks, watches, and calendars. It may also be known as the period or moment in which something happens or takes place.

How much time have you wasted? Have you been climbing up and down the same mountain day after day, year after year, wasting time? Does time really make a difference in your life? Do you consider time when you make decisions about your finances? At the precise moment you decide to make a commitment to finance something, time plays a major factor in the outcome. The time it takes to pay back that to which you have committed yourself will determine if the credit trap is controlling you.

Time can be your worst enemy, or it can work in your favor. You can let the power of time be your worst nightmare or your best friend. Time can lead you into poverty or help promote you into prosperity!

There is a thin line between poverty and prosperity, and time plays a major factor in determining which of those roads you travel. Although time is not the only factor that determines your outcome in life, it is one of the most important elements. Have you ever stopped and considered why your mortgage isn't paid off? Or why you don't have money in your retirement or savings account even though you've been working all your life?

Time waits for no one. The credit trap wants you to lose time so that poverty will continue to knock at your door. The longer you stay in the credit trap the longer you will be defeated financially. It's totally up to you to seize this moment—right now—to make things work in your favor. If the mortgage, for example, has been haunting you for the last 10 or 20 years, you must develop a strategy to pay if off early.

How many times have you said to yourself "Where did the time go?" The answer is that it's gone to others who are using it to their advantage. Lending institutions use the power of time to become wealthier. All they want is the interest you pay them. The longer they can keep you paying them the richer they get! Time works in their favor, not yours, when you make a commitment to finance something for a long period of time.

The length of time to make payments should be determined by you, not by the lending institutions. Who says you have to pay your mortgage for 30 years? Who says you have to pay on that car for 5 or 6 years? Just because your contract says the last payment is due on a certain date does not mean you have to wait until then to pay it off. You should concentrate, every day, on devising a strategy toward paying off your debts early. Time will let you choose your financial destiny if you choose to let it!

If you're reading this book, I can only assume you want time to work in your favor. Every second that passes turns into minutes; every minute becomes hours; every hour evolves into days, days into weeks, weeks into months, and infinitum. Time continues relentlessly, and for you to get out of debt and obtain the wealth and successful financial life that should be yours, you have to determine in your mind that *today* is the day that time will move over to your side.

Remember the Rule of 72 and the number of years it takes money to double? You have to find or create the rate of return that's going to yield you the best increase in the shortest length of time. The world already has its system planned. Why do you think the John Doe loan companies or the Back Street finance companies charge such high interest rates? Why are they all too happy to loan you money for a short period of time? The answer is simple: even a short period of time with the wrong interest rate and the wrong lender can be devastating to you. The sooner they can get that money back at 20% or higher, the sooner they can loan it to someone else, or even loan it to you again.

You should stay away from high interest-charging companies, because you are just wasting your time playing around with the credit trap. You're going up and down the same mountain, over and over again. That period of time during which they make you pay back your title loan could cost you as much as 50% more than it should. They give you $1,000 on your car title and then make you pay back $1,500.

You may think you're getting a deal since they didn't pull your credit report but, in reality, you are still a victim of the credit trap. Your credit was in such poor condition you had to turn to that high interest rate lender to get what you needed. These companies know that when you walk in the front door you have bad credit. The credit trap makes sure they know it.

Time is going to keep ticking whether you like it or not. That's why you should get yourself in position to move out of the credit trap. I've heard people say, over and over again, that they are surviving and holding on, but I've learned through experience that if people are just trying to survive they will always be defeated by time. Just trying to survive is a lazy person's chatter. It's negative. The bible says in Proverbs 10:4 (NIV) that lazy hands make a man poor. Going to title loan companies and other high-interest rate lenders such as cash and check advance companies are a lazy person's way of putting money in his or her pocket. That's simply a way of wasting your time (and money).

A person may think that time is something you can play around with because there's always tomorrow. And while it's true that there's always a tomorrow, letting time slip away day after day, while you're doing the same old lazy, life-defeating things, is dangerous to your finances. Your enemy—debt—has plenty of time to play with you.

Just surviving each day, barely getting by, and allowing the cycle of waking and sleeping to define you, permits the time that has been entrusted to you to fade away. Every human being has the same amount of time each day, but those who say, "Yes I'm surviving and holding on" are in a trance—actually a trap—that's holding them back from prospering. Individuals who talk this way are not just being held back financially, but in every area of their lives.

You must begin to look at time as a way to strive not just only to survive and make the most of every moment! When making a decision about your finances, or anything else in life, you should always think about future consequences and not just immediate gratification. Cast the "just surviving" mentality out of your mind and begin to strive for success!

If the credit trap is calling your name and telling you to go to that Back Street loan company, you have to respond to that evil spirit and say "I am striving for better than that!" Your time is too valuable to be wasted on decisions that will continue to haunt you, hold you back, and keep you below the achievement bar.

I have spoken with people who lived their lives going from one Check Advance Company to the next. Week after week, they paid off one with money from the other, each time falling deeper and deeper into the trap. Before these people knew it, so much time had passed and that hole seemed too deep for them to climb out. I remember telling them that they didn't get into this mess overnight and they wouldn't get out of it overnight, but if they wanted to they *could* climb out!

The good news is that tomorrow is a new day and a new day means a fresh start. Time can work in your favor if you stand up for a better quality of life! Don't just settle for anything that comes your way. Begin to realize that if you fall for everything you stand for nothing. Stand up for the good things in your financial walk, and not for every new thing that comes your way. So what if there's a new title loan company or finance company on every street corner? Just drive right by without so much as a second thought. Your time is too precious to be wasted on nonsense.

Whether you acknowledge it or not, it is time for you to take a stand for your more abundant life! Time will continue to pass whether or not you change your way of living, whether or not you create a plan to pay off your debts and whether or not you decide to stop borrowing money. Time will always continue to tick and be a factor in the decisions you make. Don't waste your time any longer!

CHAPTER TWELVE

IMPULSE BUYING

Impulse buying is another form of credit trapping, especially if you are charging your purchases. Before buying anything on impulse, and charging it, you should always think about future consequences. For example, is it worth paying for an $85 dress for 9 months or longer on credit? That's about how long it would take to pay it off if you made the minimum payments. Use your wisdom and think about the future consequences before you jump into any impulse decision.

And don't let your children push you into buying on impulse! Your children can lead you into the credit trap quickly and without thinking. Your kids don't mean you any harm, but they don't know any better. It's your job to apply wisdom and teach them the truth.

When children see an item that they want immediately, check out all the details, think about it, and then use good judgment. If you decide to purchase it, don't say "charge it" pay cash. Don't let the excitement of the moment lead you into financing your future away and falling into the credit trap. The spirit of debt will use anything to try to trick you, even your children!

Even if you're paying cash, impulse buying is still not a good idea. God tells us to be anxious for nothing. This means be patient! When you get to the point of living a cash-paying lifestyle, you have to be twice as smart. The spirit of debt would like nothing better than to see you hurting for cash and borrowing money again. But you have to be smarter by always planning ahead. A person who fails to plan, plans to fail. And this is true even after you are debt-free!

Make a decision *right now* to stop buying and borrowing on impulse and live a cash-buying lifestyle forever. Renew your mind and begin to pay off what you already have. Be patient; tell money and debt you will not be a slave to them and do not allow impulse buying to control you or your financial future.

CONTROL YOUR SPENDING

You will not be increased financially if you're always overspending. Taking care of what God allows you to receive is an important part of your earthly journey. How you handle money will determine how much God will allow into your hands. It's called being a good steward!

God will not bless you abundantly if He knows you are not making wise decisions with what He is already allowing you to have. Ask yourself: can God trust me with more than enough? What would I do with more than enough?

God is looking for someone He can pour His resources into to make a difference in this world. That's why you're still here. He's giving you another chance. God wants someone He can trust to handle His money properly: someone who knows how to tithe . . . and budget . . . and sow good seeds . . . and invest to make a good return. Is that you? Can God trust you? Can you control your spending and be a good and faithful servant?

Stop wasting money trying to satisfy your flesh. If you are spending money out of control, you will never have more than enough. You'll keep borrowing and borrowing, you'll try get-rich-quick schemes, you'll continually seek money, and some people will want it so much as to even steal it!

This is just where the enemy wants you; broke, busted and disgusted. But just remember that God sent His son Jesus to give you life, and life more abundantly. In other words, He wants to restore you back to your wealthy place. After all, that's where you belong!

Begin to tell money to work for you! Tell money you're in control! Seek God first and His righteousness and **all** these things will be added unto you. Including money! Control your spending and you won't have to live in a land of lack and want. Instead, you'll rule in your dominion and be found faithful when Jesus returns!

> **Impulse buying and uncontrolled spending will keep you in debt!**

CHAPTER THIRTEEN

INSURANCE

Let's look at the effects of life insurance and how it can make or break a family.

Not having insurance—or even buying the wrong type—can be devastating to your family's future. The breadwinner should have enough life insurance to cover 10 years of his or her income in the event of death. While we all hope that early or sudden death won't occur, it is something that could happen. But by having the right type and amount of insurance your family won't have to struggle to make ends meet.

There have been many cases where there was no insurance on the one who died and the family had to borrow money to pay for funeral expenses and to make ends meet. It's sad to say but the credit trap is always waiting to pull you in even when death occurs. I urge you to take the time to protect your family by making sure you and your spouse are adequately insured.

If the breadwinner is underinsured it can have major negative effects on the lifestyle of the survivors. But if the right amount of insurance has been acquired, it can be very helpful to the remaining family members. Mortgages can be paid in full, college education can still occur, and other debts can be paid off also. Death does not have to destroy your financial lifestyle if the right amount of insurance has been provided.

There are many types of insurance policies available to consumers and choosing the best one for you and your family can be confusing. My advice is to "keep it simple," which is why *term* life insurance is usually the best, you will get more for your money.

Whole life insurance is often what insurance salespeople push. They tell you that you can save money and have life insurance in the same policy. But you must be careful with policies that offer you savings or retirement plans as well as death benefits. Normally, the premiums are so high that you can only afford enough insurance to barely cover funeral costs and, in some cases, not enough to cover that cost.

Another downfall to this type of policy is that in the first few years, no money (or very little money, at best) goes toward the savings plan that is suppose to be attached to this type of policy. And when you die, they often don't give your beneficiary any money you actually accumulated. These are just a few of the negative reasons why you should never buy insurance and a savings plan in the same policy.

My philosophy is very simple: You buy life insurance for when you die and you save money for when you live. The reality is that you can't live and die at the same time. That's why I recommend term insurance to provide your family with a death benefit, and a *separate* saving and/or investment plan. With separate plans, your family gets both the insurance benefit and the money you saved!

Term insurance is *all* life insurance, with no additives. Normally, the premiums are relatively inexpensive and you can afford well over the payout that will cover funeral costs and leave your beneficiary with plenty of additional money. With the amount of coverage you can get from term insurance, your family should be able to continue life with less stress and financial headaches in the event of death.

Life insurance companies actually bank on you living for a long time; that's how they get rich. The longer you pay your monthly premiums, the richer they get. If everybody were to die quickly, the insurers would go broke from paying death benefits. Chances are you will live a long time and the insurance companies know this. But it's your job to outsmart them by buying the right type of life insurance and having the right type of savings/investments accounts. The ultimate goal is to eventually have enough money saved over a period of time so you won't need to continue to carry life insurance if you choose to drop your policy. But this should only be done if you have an abundance amount of money saved for your immediate family in the event of death.

Life insurance is less expensive when you're younger and this is when you should purchase your policy. Parents will usually keep a child covered under their policy until the child is out of the home and on his or her own. Children are covered by what is called a child rider under there parents policy.

At an age of 27, a high amount of insurance is affordable with the right type of policy. For example, a person who earns $40,000 a year should be insured for a minimum of $400,000 in term life insurance. In the event of an untimely death, this amount of insurance should be enough to pay not only funeral expenses, but your mortgage, children's college educations, other small debts, and have some left over for your survivors to re-invest for future use.

Using the same $400,000 life insurance policy, let's assume you are investing money in some type of program outside of your policy (which is what you should be doing). Assume also that at retirement age you have $400,000 or more saved in cash and your mortgage is already paid off, college expenses are over, the car is paid for, and there are no other major obligations. Now you have an option: You can either cancel your life insurance policy because you have enough money saved in the event of death, or you could keep the insurance policy for added wealth. The good news is that now you have a choice.

The problem is that most people at retirement age don't have the chance to choose because they bought the wrong type of life insurance policy and they didn't save enough money. But even if you saved $200,000 at retirement you are still better off than the person who didn't save anything and had the wrong type of insurance policy.

People have been taught to believe that all they need is enough life insurance for funeral expenses and nothing more left over for their families. What they fail to realize is that, after paying premiums on a policy with a face amount of only $5,000 for 20 to 30 years, they have paid more for the insurance amount than what the policy is worth. If you pay $40 a month in premiums for 25 years, you would spend $12,000 for a $5,000 life insurance policy! This is what you typically get with a whole life insurance policy. High premiums with a low face amount of insurance, and this is a waste of your time and money.

When you think of life insurance you should be thinking high face amount with low premiums. This is typically what you can get with a term life insurance policy.

Buying the right type of life insurance policy and investing the difference can create wealth for your family—including the next generation. You need a lot more than "just enough" to cover funeral costs. You need enough to pay for the funeral and then to have an abundance left over!

CHAPTER FOURTEEN

HOW TO BUY A CAR AND
NOT GET RIPPED OFF

No one wants to be ripped off when buying a car, but it happens every day. Automobile dealerships make billions of dollars every year from people who are not knowledgeable about buying a vehicle. It's so true when the bible says we suffer because of lack of knowledge!

I want to give you some advice so your next car-buying experience won't be a bad one. Just remember that your ultimate goal is to pay cash and live a cash lifestyle. However, if you haven't yet reached that point and you need to finance a vehicle, finance smartly so the credit trap won't hold you back!

First of all, never, and I mean NEVER pay sticker or asking price for a new or used vehicle. There is **always** room for the dealership to negotiate the price of a vehicle.

DO NOT go to a car dealership with a payment mentality. For example, never say, "If you can get my payments to $450 or no more than $500 a month I will buy this car today!" Never think this way and never say this. While your focus is on a *payment*, dealerships focus on a *price*. They will love you to death if you come to them with that attitude, and you will surely be ripped off (as a lot of people already have been).

The dealerships make their profit on the sales price, not on the monthly payment you make. The financial institution that finances your vehicle sends the dealership a check for the price you agreed to buy the car for. Your monthly payments will go to the credit institution that finances the vehicle for you. The dealership does not care about what your monthly payments may be, because they don't have to make them. You do!

That's why it is your job to negotiate the price of the vehicle down to as low as possible and/or even down to the invoice. Again, NEVER say "If you can get my payments to a certain amount, I will buy this vehicle." You are just setting yourself up for the credit trap to pull you in with payments higher and longer than they really should be.

Focus on the price of the vehicle and don't be afraid to talk the salesperson down on the price. God does not give you the spirit of fear! If you have to finance, remember that if the price of the vehicle you are buying is negotiated down to as low as possible, your payments will probably be lower than you anticipated.

Know your budget before you go to the dealership. Stay within or, better yet, stay *below* your limit. Buying too much of a car could result in a financial disaster. It doesn't make sense to look good in a new car for five or six months and then give it back because you couldn't afford the payments. Don't set yourself up for failure. Know what you can afford before you get to the dealership.

Never buy a vehicle on impulse! Always check for incentives on the vehicle you are considering before you get to the dealership. Most of the time, the manufacturer of the vehicle (not the dealership, but the maker of the vehicle) will give cash back (rebates) to the buyer of a vehicle. It is your job to do your homework *before arriving at the dealership* to insure that you'll get the best price and all the incentives (rebates and other offers) that may be available to you.

Dealerships sell in volume. They have a goal each month to sell a certain amount of vehicles. Some manufacturers will give the dealerships a kickback if they sell more of a certain model. This is a good way for you to get a good deal, but only if you know what the incentives are. (Please see the back of this book for a list of vehicle manufacturer's phone numbers.)

If you want even a better deal, buy the vehicle you want in the last few days of the month! Make it the last day, if you're bold enough! This will put you in better control of the deal. The sales person and the dealership will be more open to give you the deal you want. They can sell you a unit and move on to the next customer before the month is out, or before the business day is over. Remember, they sell in volume and it's a game to them—but it's *your* money!

Try buying at the end of the month on your next vehicle purchase and you'll be amazed not only at the deal you'll get, but at the difference in the sales person and dealership attitudes.

So when does buying a vehicle fall under the credit trap guidelines? When you finance it! I know that financing a vehicle is very common but it still falls under the credit trap guidelines. Remember, it's the world's way of doing business when you buy now and pay later.

A $20,000 car can cost you an extra $4,000-$7,000 dollars when you finance it (depending on the interest rate). This is money wasted and given into the credit trap. I realize this is common to the world's system for financing a vehicle, but God's way is uncommon to the world. His system is better! It's a system of owing no man nothing but love.

So save your money and pay cash! Sell your current car when you're ready to purchase a different car and apply the money you've saved with the money you made on selling your old car, and pay cash! Be anxious for nothing! You must get out of the world's system of financing vehicles or financing anything for that matter.

The credit trap, which I believe is straight from the devil, wants you to be in debt and stay in debt forever. But God wants you to be free, and free for life! He came to give you a more abundant life. He didn't say anything about a more in debt life!

It has to start with you. And then you have to teach your children to do the same. It feels so much better to drive a nice car and own it, free and clear, with no strings attached. I'm talking about having the title to it! That's real ownership and dominion. Having life abundantly could be defined as having a Mercedes Benz, but having life **more** abundantly could be defined as, having a Mercedes Benz and the title to it!

No payments will eventually equal more abundance and that's what Jesus came to give us: life and life *more **abundantly!***

You see, the world wants you to think as it does. The world's system says make payments, don't pay cash, because in three to five years the body style of this car will change anyway any you can do a trade in. That's the trick of the enemy, to keep you in the credit trap and financing a new car every three to five years.

And you're taught that if your neighbor or co-worker has a new car, you should have one, also. It's okay to have it, but have it the right way. Pay cash and get the title, that's real abundance! Don't let fear keep you from entering into the next realm of prosperity!

If you make $30,000 a year ($2,500 a month before taxes) and you save $500 a month, in just three years you'll have $18,000! If you save $500 for 5 years that's $30,000 plus interest. And remember the "Rule of 72" from chapter one? So don't tell me you can't pay cash for a new car. If you want something you've never had, you've got to do something you've never done!

The credit trap doesn't have power over you any longer. Start saving now to pay cash! Use your dominion and stay in control. Decree and claim your cash-buying lifestyle *today*. Speak it, believe it, have it and, most of all, eventually you'll have it debt-free!

Grow into your wealthy place by staying out of the trap!

CHAPTER FIFTEEN

STAYING FOCUSED

There are many distractions and obstacles in the world in which we live. And many of them appear in our lives when we make a commitment to do something great. One of them, of course, is the credit trap, and I won't kid you: it's not easy to establish total freedom from the credit trap.

Just remember that if everything in life came easy, everybody would have exactly what they wanted when they wanted it. Instead, you'll have to fight for most good things. The race is not given to the strong; it is given to the one who endures! Being strong in body and spirit is good, but if you don't have persistence you won't win.

You must stay focused on your goal of becoming completely debt-free and out of the credit trap. Staying focused doesn't mean you won't have setbacks, because you probably will. It asks how bad you want it. It asks if you can keep your eye on the prize. If getting out of the credit trap is easy, it might not be worth achieving . . . and if it's easy to accomplish you would probably be out of it already.

As I said earlier, the world's system is designed to keep you in debt. It wants you to borrow money for everything, giving you the impression that credit is the answer. If you want something, they ask, "How much money do you need to borrow?" You must reprogram yourself to start thinking like a lender and not like a borrower. The borrower will always be a slave to the lender because you will always have payments to make. I know it will take time to overcome debt and borrowing, but you must start thinking differently to achieve what you really want.

If you never break the cycle of borrowing money you will never be free from the credit trap! Making a decision to get out of the trap requires determination and hard work. Once you really make up in your mind that this enemy can no longer hold you captive, your race begins. Your strategy must be implemented and your mind must be focused on the finish line.

The only way you loose or fail is if you quit. It takes a lot of endurance to win this kind of race because, as you run your race, the enemy of debt is going to try to pull you down every chance it gets. But don't focus on the debt; keep your focus on the grand prize. And if you continue to run—even with that debt monkey on your back—eventually the burden will get lighter and lighter!

While winning may seem hard, you must realize that failing is easy. To fail, all you have to do is quit. Nobody really wants to fail, but trying to win can seem so daunting that it can shut down your belief system. I believe a lot of people are afraid of winning, because to be a winner requires courage, strength and determination. You may be wondering what you will do when you reach the finish line. Or, what you will do when you have no payments and extra cash, and you become the lender.

Fear will keep you from winning and lead you to failure! In order to win, you have to see yourself as a winner. Stop telling yourself that this is the way it's supposed to be. Being in debt and in the credit trap is not God's will for your life! Don't allow your thinking to keep you trapped and living as a borrower.

Staying focused means you have to think as if you are already crossing the finish line. It means you know in your mind and heart that you have already won! For you, the finish line could be paying off your car early. To someone else, it could be to own a car lot. Whatever the finish line means to you, just remember that when you cross it you have to be prepared for the next level you are entering. Just because your car is paid off or you opened that car lot doesn't mean the race has ended and you've arrived at your destiny.

Rest if you must, but you can't stop there. This achievement in your life will only cause more obstacles to show up in your path. Now you have to be twice as smart and even more focused to keep what you have earned!

CHAPTER SIXTEEN

CREDIT IS NOT THE SOLUTION

The world's system pushes the use of credit so hard that you would almost think living debt-free is impossible. But that's not true. You can live a cash lifestyle! Change the way you think and you will change your future. Borrowing money can be avoided when you put yourself in the proper mental position.

Let me tell you a short story about how, years ago, I used to think credit was the answer. At one time in my life, I thought that all I needed to do was borrow $800. That's right, the princely sum of $800. I thought this would solve all my problems in the world. I had no major debt, but I thought I really needed this $800 for some reason or another.

I had no established credit, and I tried everything I could to get this money. Finally I got the loan and, to my surprise, the money was gone in a matter of days. I realized that my problems—and I don't even remember what they were—had gotten a little worse since I now had to repay this loan and had nothing to show for it.

I tried to borrow more money to make me feel better, so I could say I had something. Ignorant of the facts, I could only see my immediate wants, which were cash and more cash. I wasn't even considering what the future consequences would be from continuous borrowing, so I borrowed again and again. I thought this money would solve all my problems, but I didn't have a clue as to what I was getting myself into.

As time passed, my financial decisions were driving me to rock bottom. Still ignorant of the facts, I thought credit was the answer to my problems. And since I was in the credit game, I continued to consistently borrow money, which was beginning to create a real problem in my life. At this point, I guess you could say I was addicted to credit . . . and it was so easy to get it.

I didn't know how to say no. I was in over my head and I was sinking fast. My thinking was messed up and I could only think about how I could get the next loan hoping that, this time, things would be different. Well, guess what? Things were not different. The only thing that had changed was that I had fallen deeper into the credit trap.

I was stuck in debt and it was draining me financially, physically and spiritually. And now I really had a major problem. This may be how you are feeling right now! I was there, and I know it's not a good feeling. But I want you to know that if I was able to climb my way out, so can you. It starts in your mind!

Change the way you think right now and ask God to renew your mind! Don't rely on credit to solve your problems; instead, rely on the word of God. Just because your credit is good doesn't mean credit is good for you. God is the way, the truth, and the life." You may ask:

> *What way?* The way to your wealth, because God gives you power to get wealth!

> *What truth?* It shall come to pass if you follow all His commandments that you will be the lender and not the borrower!

> *What life?* The life of more abundance!

Seek His Kingdom's principles first, and everything else will line up through your good planning and obedience!

If you think that credit is always the answer, you can void and cancel the word of God in your life concerning true financial prosperity. You have to choose today whom you will serve: the lender or God? If you choose God, He will give you the power to get more than enough. Because **He is a God of more than enough!**

I want you to know that credit is **not** the answer to your financial dreams. It is merely the answer to all of your financial nightmares if you misuse it. I am not saying you won't ever have to use credit, but I am saying that, eventually, there should come a time in your life that you put an end to borrowing money so you can walk into your true prosperity that is already yours.

You can start right now. Begin to move toward living outside of the credit trap. Your financial future will be the result of the decisions you make today. If credit has called your name for a long time and you are in the trap, begin to dig your way out one bill at a time!

IS IT CALLING YOUR NAME?

Television is loaded with commercials for borrowing money, refinancing mortgages, transferring high interest credit cards to other credit cards, and many other money-lending procedures. But this is nothing more than the credit trap calling your name trying to keep you in debt.

Some lending institutions even have the nerve to tell you to get out of debt by consolidating your current debts. What a crazy idea! How can you get out of debt by renewing your debt on a different loan? It doesn't work that way. You are still in debt, just to another lender. By consolidating your loans without a purpose and plan to accelerate the payoff could be devastating to you.

What I mean is that if you are not disciplined, you could very easily fall into a bigger trap than before you consolidated. Consolidation could work in your favor, if managed properly. And it could put you in control by focusing on one debt instead of many. But remember, Satan is crafty, so you have to be wiser than any debt you have or are tempted by.

Don't let it control you. Instead, you can control it by paying extra towards the principal, making double payments, paying lump sums to the principal at tax time and, if you're exceptionally disciplined, you can make half payments every two weeks. For example, if your monthly payment is $500, pay $250 every two weeks, instead. This strategy by itself will accelerate your loan for a very quick payoff! You could save as much as five years or more on a 30-year mortgage by applying the every-two-week principle!

The world's system paints a tempting picture that sells debt. And that's exactly what they're doing: selling money to keep you in debt! Competing between each other as to who has the best loan or the best interest rate. One tells you that their money is better than some other lending institution's money. How can their money be better? Money is money. A $100 bill at your bank is the same as a $100 bill at my bank. But if you listen to the advertisements, you would think that money is different from lender to lender.

They say you can live a better life if you borrow their money. I've heard it and I've seen it and if you've paid close attention, so have you. It doesn't matter which advertisement it is or where you borrow it from. Just remember that debt comes to steal, kill and destroy your life financially, mentally and spiritually! Don't let it happen to you or your children.

Beloved reader, you are more in control of your destiny than you think. See yourself the king that you are created to be. Debt can hold you captive and in fear only if you do not command it what to do. Have you ever been to or seen a circus where the trainer tames a lion? As big and bad as that lion seems, it won't dare harm the trainer as long as the trainer shows authority and no fear. This is how we should be concerning money. Don't be afraid of it. Tame it and make it do as you speak!

There's another big hype out there known as *credit scores*. Everywhere you turn you are asked, "What is your credit score," or "How high is your credit score?" It's true that if your credit score is very high you will, most likely, get the best interest rates. But if you truly want out of the credit trap don't let the credit score hype keep you in the loop of borrowing money!

There has to come a time in your life that enough is enough, no matter how good your credit score is! Start the process of getting out of debt and staying out of debt, and then your credit score won't be an issue because you'll be living a cash lifestyle!

And then there's Internet borrowing. You can borrow money online in seconds. What a convenient way to borrow. Or, should I say, how convenient it is to fall into the credit trap! Internet borrowing is just another avenue to keep you in the cycle of borrowing, but in an easier and more convenient way. I'm sure you can see that this is nothing other than a trick of the enemy. You have to remember that the world's system of credit is designed to keep you in debt and get as much in interest payments as possible, even if it is over the internet.

Don't be lured in by those fancy banners and pop-ups ads that say "Quick approval online in seconds." Those few seconds of credit approval can turn your future into a nightmare of everlasting debt.

Money borrowed must be paid back. If a person has $300,000 in cash and assets and owes $300,000 on loans and notes, that person's net worth is $0. What good is it to have $300,000 and owe $300,000 plus interest? But if a person has acquired $300,000 in cash and assets and owes no man anything but love, then he or she truly has a net worth of $300,000! That's the way God wants you have it, with no strings attached!

Remember, nothing happens overnight, but if you follow God's commands it shall come to pass that you will lend and not borrow! Deuteronomy 28:1&12 KJV.

> Borrowing money must become a thing of the past!

VEHICLE MANUFACTURER PHONE NUMBERS

ACURA	800-299-1009
ALFA ROMEO	800-255-6727
AMERICAN HONDA MOTORS	800-999-1009
AMERICAN ISUZU MOTORS	800-934-0934
AUDI	800-955-5100
BMW	800-831-1117
CHRYSLER CORPORATION	800-992-1997
DAIHATSU	800-777-7070
FERRARI	201-816-2652
FORD MOTOR COMPANY	800-392-3673
GENERAL MOTORS	800-521-7300
CADILLAC	800-458-8006
CHEVROLET/GEO	800-222-1020
OLDSMOBILE	800-422-6537
PONTIAC	800-762-2737
SATURN	800-553-6000
HYUNDAI	800-663-5151
JAGUAR	800-452-4827
MAZDA	800-222-5500
MERCEDES BENZ	800-222-0100
MITSUBISHI MOTORS	800-222-0037
NISSAN MOTORS	800-647-7261
PEUGEOT	800-345-5549
PORSCHE	800-545-8039

SAAB   800-955-9007
SUBARU   800-782-2783
TOYOTA MOTORS   800-331-4331
VOLVO   800-458-1552

www.ingramcontent.com/pod-product-compliance
Lightning Source LLC
Chambersburg PA
CBHW022121170526
45157CB00004B/1711

9 781425 766979